NANCE:

TRIALS OF THE FIRST SLAVE FREED BY ABRAHAM LINCOLN

A TRUE STORY OF NANCE LEGINS-COSTLEY

STORY BY

CARL ADAMS

ART BY

LANI JOHNSON

Lincoln, Abraham. 2. Illinois History. 3. Slavery. 4. Biography.

ISBN: 1502947595
ISBN: 9781502947598

LCCN: 2013914435
LCCN Imprint Name: North Pekin, Illinois

CURATOR AFRICAN AMERICAN MUSEUM: Peoria, Illinois: "At that time, what black woman had a lawyer to take her case to court? She was thought of as the first civil rights leader as a black woman because she did stand up for the fact that she thought she should be free. And she went to court five times...she was persistent."

Ms Millie Hall

NPR RADIO: "Lincoln was wise enough to know that once you set a precedent, future laws will be based upon that precedent. Lincoln is able to get the court to say that people cannot be bought, sold, traded... Once it became clear in the eyes of the law...in Illinois, that means that slavery effectively will die."

Dr. Junius Rodriquez, author of
CHRONOLOGY OF WORLD
SLAVERY

JOURNAL OF THE ILLINOIS STATE HISTORICAL SOCIETY: "This is the only story about Abraham Lincoln that is really new...Carl Adams has unearthed an obscure case Lincoln tried before the Illinois State Supreme Court. The case illustrates that the legal ground work for Lincoln's views on slavery was laid much earlier than many scholars have assumed."

Dr. Eileen McMahon, Editor

NPR RADIO: "She was born in the building used as the Territorial Capitol, on site where the 1818 Constitution was written which prohibited slavery, yet she was held in bondage... The polarity of that is just absolutely amazing!"

William Maddox, History teacher at
Lincoln middle school, Peoria, Illinois

"This was probably the first time he [Lincoln] gave to these grave questions [on slavery] so full and elaborate an investigation...it is not improbable that the study of this case deepened and developed the antislavery convictions of his just and generous mind."

Congressman Isaac Arnold, 1881

"It was next to impossible for a Judge to detect an error in any grounds that he assumed in argument. Admitting his premises his conclusions were irresistible."

Judge Thomas, 1866

"Among the cases...of dramatic import... 'that she had declared herself to be free.'"

Ida Tarbell, 1902

"Of his conduct of this case Mr. Lincoln was more or less proud, and the case itself has been generously and frequently cited in the appellate courts of other states."

Jessie Weik, 1922

"For nearly a century it has been storied and sung that Lincoln, as a young man, won freedom for Black Nance, a slave..."

W.H. Williamson, 1938

"Lincoln argued, in part, that the girl was a free person until she was proven to be a slave...The Supreme Court took practically the same view and Lincoln won his case."

Carl Sandberg, 1947

"Certainly this was one of the most far-reaching of the 250 cases in which Lincoln was to appear before the state's highest tribunal."

Justice William O. Douglas, 1963

Dedication

This work is dedicated to the living relatives of Nance and Benjamin Legins-Costley who have since melted into the American fabric. It is also dedicated to the living grandchildren and great-grandchildren of Nance's children: Amanda Costley-Lewis; Elisa Jane; William Henry Costley; Mary Costley-Ashby; Leander "Dote" Costley, who married Sadie Chaffers in 1876; Harriet Costley-Taylor; Eliza Ann; James Costley; and all other relatives, wherever they may be.

Through the years of research it seems over a hundred people have contributed something to the revelations of this story, which had been lost to history.

I'd like to acknowledge the wonderful staffs of the following institutions: the public libraries of Peoria, Pekin, Evanston, and Springfield, Illinois; the Sangamon Valley collections; the Illinois Historical library; the Wesley City Historical Society; Tazewell County Genealogical Society; Illinois Regional Archive Depository, University of Illinois, Springfield; Illinois State Historical Society; and the Abraham Lincoln Association.

Thanks to artist Lani Johnson for the artwork; Terence Goggin and William Maddox for computer support; assistance from Jadi Campbell and Andrea Ariman and for my children's patience Abigail, Audrey, Andrea, Luke, and Amy for reading, encouraging, and advising.

Introduction

Nance Costley, circa 1813-1873, the First Slave Freed by Abraham Lincoln

One of the first lessons American grade school children learn about US history is that the Civil War was caused by sectional conflict over the slavery issue. The nineteenth-century historians called Lincoln "The Great Emancipator." However, some late twentieth-century writers challenged that long-held belief, and some black writers have claimed Lincoln never freed a single slave and even went so far as to call Lincoln a "racist."

Late twentieth-century American history also witnessed a number of race riots and hate crimes. In the mid-1990s, a short local-history story appeared in a Tazewell County, Illinois, newspaper with only four facts: A "Negro girl named Nance" was the first slave freed by Abraham Lincoln through the legal case of *Bailey v. Cromwell* in 1841. But that was it; that was *all of it*. No one seemed to have written anything else about her in over a hundred years! What struck me the most was that the date was a full twenty years before the Civil War. I then realized I had moved to the Illinois county which Nance had lived for over forty years, so there had to be county records. I hoped a true story of Nance would benefit race relations.

WHO WAS NANCE? Where did she come from? Did she know Lincoln? What became of her after freedom? The nerve of her! What possessed her to try the nearly impossible? There are over 10,000 major works on Lincoln; and this is the only one about the slave who started Lincoln on the path that changed American History

About the same time, a cousin published my family's genealogy. As I read and researched, I saw a difference between nineteenth-century and twentieth-century historical biographies. Nineteenth-century histories included family genealogies, but twentieth-century biographies did not. A biography was missing from the story of Nance Legins-Costley. No one knew much of anything about the principal people involved in Nance's life, times, and trials.

What I also discovered during this research was that my family did more than farming. Since my grandfather was orphaned at five years old, I simply didn't know that I had a unique heritage of lawyers, politicians, genealogists, and historians on both sides of my family. On my father's side of my family was Henry Adams, a historian and Thomas Adams, a genealogist. On my mother's side was John C. Moses, Illinois historian from Winchester.

It also surprised me to learn that I was related to conductors of the Underground Railroad, I also discovered that I am a distant cousin of President John Q. Adams, who, while in Congress--just like Abraham Lincoln--was antislavery but insisted he was not an abolitionist. Both won historic slavery cases: Adams won *United States v. Amistad* in 1841, and just five months later, Abraham Lincoln won *Bailey v. Cromwell*. Both of these men were avid newspaper readers and probably knew of each other's cases in supreme court. This historical coincidence is not included in any other book.

So just how did these forebears help me to understand Nance's story? Cousin Henry, the historian, solved one mystery when he wrote in his *The History of the United States of America* in 1889, "No good historian was ever a good lawyer. Whether any good lawyer could be a good historian might be equally doubted." I tested this idea during my research and found that it was also true in the twenty-first century. Historians didn't grasp the significance of the legal side of the story, and lawyers could not understand the importance of history.

Cousin Thomas, a genealogist, showed me that love of American principles of justice and independent political thought were deeply rooted in my family. When the story got difficult and frustrating, Cousin John Quincy's determination with the Amistad slaves was inspiring. John Moses from my mother's family wrote the Illinois history of the people and times of Nance's life.

Even though for more than 150 years, no one published her name as Nance Legins-Costley, Nance herself was and still is an inspiration of determination and empowerment. She struggled to overcome great odds for the sake of her children, both born and unborn. To Lincoln's credit, he took a case other lawyers would have thought unwinnable; she had lost in the supreme court twice before.

But, history is so boring, right? That depends on how the subject is presented. Now, let's consider the notion that Lincoln was a racist. Consider the following facts, which no one else has presented in this manner. Lincoln's barber was a black man in Springfield named William Fleurville. These men were so close that Lincoln entrusted Billy the Barber with the care of his best friend, his dog Fido, while Lincoln was in Washington. And the iconic beard Lincoln wore during the White House years was not a common style at the time but was designed with the help of black Billy the Barber. Think about this: if Abraham Lincoln was racist in word or deed during the 1850s, while campaigning for the Senate and the White House, would he really have been stupid enough to allow a Negro man to stand behind him on a regular basis with a sharp, straightedge razor cutting at his throat? I think not!

Carl Adams, Pekin, Illinois 2010

A Timeline of How Slavery and Abolition Shaped
Illinois Law in the Nineteenth Century

1800:   Indiana Territory, including Illinois, created by Congress; Gabriel's slave revolt near Richmond, Virginia, spread fear and harsh black laws.

1803:   Governor William Harrison passed "indentured servitude," a form of slavery, eventually creating Illinois and Indiana as the only two indentured states in the nineteenth century.

1809:   Illinois Territory created by Congress; indentured servitude continued; Abraham Lincoln born in a humble log cabin in Kentucky.

1813:   Nance born to slaves Randol and Anachy Legins in a large guesthouse that hosts the Illinois territorial government, owned by Captain Thomas Cox.

1817:   General Assembly bill to abolish servitude vetoed by Governor Ninian Edwards.

1818:   Illinois statehood initiated a congressional debate over the number of slave states versus free states, which was settled with the Missouri Compromise of 1820.

1822:   Illinois' first abolitionist governor, Edward Coles, elected; Thomas Cox (now a colonel) chaired committee to make slavery permanent law. News spread of Denmark Vesey slave revolt.

1825:   State bank failed; Cox, a daily drunk and bankrupt, mortgaged Nance and Dice.

1826:   The state bank, Sheriff Taylor, and Nathan Cromwell sued Cox, who lost in court.

1827:   Nance's auction was tested in the supreme court case, *Nance, a Woman of Color v. John Howard*.

1828:   The case was tried again as *Nance, a girl of Color v. Howard*. Nance lost, re-establishing indentured servitude.

1831:   Nat Turner slave revolt threatened Richmond, Virginia; England abolished slavery.

1832:   Black Hawk Indian war involved Cox, Lincoln, Bailey, and Cromwell.

1836: Nance, now mother-to-be, sold to Bailey by her master Nathan who died at age 65; Nance asserted freedom.

1837: Bailey signed petition of Illinois Antislavery Society, and anti-abolition riots began.

1839: Cromwell's son sued Bailey; Bailey lost in court and retained Lincoln to appeal.

1840: Nance Cromwell married Benjamin Costley; Lincoln appealed to supreme court.

1841: In *Bailey v. Cromwell*, Bailey, Nance, and Lincoln won an "unwinnable" slavery case.

1845: Illinois Supreme Court outlawed all forms of slavery in the state.

1848: Illinois made all slavery unconstitutional.

1865: Lincoln signed the Thirteenth Amendment: "Neither slavery nor involuntary servitude shall exist..."

NANCE:

TRIALS OF THE FIRST SLAVE
FREED BY ABRAHAM LINCOLN

I

Abraham Lincoln's first Illinois Supreme Court session involved one of his most important law cases—a case against slavery. Lincoln pleaded for liberty from slavery for a black woman, Nance Legins-Costley, and her three children, twenty years before the Civil War.

Loopholes in Illinois law created "indentured servitude," a disguise for slavery that allowed Nance and a thousand others to be held in "involuntary servitude." In winning the case of *Bailey v. Cromwell* in 1841, Lincoln repeated three times a fifty-year-old idea that, "Neither slavery nor involuntary servitude shall exist."[1]

The weather was hot and humid in July 1841 in Springfield, Illinois. As Abraham arranged and rearranged the quills, paper, and ink well, he was a little worried his nervousness would show through to the justices. Abraham's long hands were jittery as he wiped beads of sweat from his forehead. Then he felt the jagged scar just under his hairline, reminding him he had a personal reason for hating slavery. The scar brought back memories of when, at age nineteen, Lincoln had been attacked, clubbed on the head, and almost killed by runaway slaves along the Mississippi River. Twitching nerves suddenly gave way to firm determination. Slavery was violence!

Bailey v. Cromwell had been in legal appeals for five years, as long as Abraham had been a lawyer. When Lincoln read the case history, he studied old court documents showing the trials of Nance had gone as far back as 1826. The court records showed that Nance had hungered for her own "personal liberty" for over fifteen years.[2]

Since Lincoln had been appointed as legal *guardian* for orphans several times in his law career and had lost his own mother at age ten, he may have had sympathy for Black orphans whose mother had been sold away from her young children in 1820.

II

The Cox family was moving. Nance Legins-Cox, an African American servant, and her younger sister, Dice, were trained to do their work serving the public by Mrs. Roba and Grandmother Jane in the Cox boarding house across the street from the Illinois state capitol building in Vandalia. A state senator and militia colonel, Thomas Cox was an important man; he was the US Registrar of the Federal Land Office and owned the Hotel Columbia under the sign of George Washington. Cox was responsible for moving the capitol from Kaskaskia to Vandalia. Next, he planned to use his influence to move the capitol again to the center of the state, to Springfield, and maybe make a run for governor.

One could assume that an illiterate slave would know very little. Even though Nance was but five years old in 1818 when the Illinois Constitution was written in her home, she grew up in the commercial boarding house where public issues were openly discussed. The leading issues of the day were land titles and slavery, and her owner Colonel Thomas Cox served as one of the first state senators from 1818-1822. During the 1822 General Assembly, Cox was named chairman of the convention committee, intent on making Illinois a perpetual slave state by constitutional amendment. And Nance was listening.

Illinois in the 1820s was a state of pure air, crystal clear water, and virgin soil that seemed to grow everything well. The Coxes loaded a large prairie wagon with their four small children and servants, put their furnishings onto an ox cart, and set out on a seventy mile trip across the Grand Prairie to a tiny crossroads hamlet, Springfield, named for its fields of many small springs at home-building sites. The village, only three blocks long with buildings lining only one street—from First to Third along Jefferson Avenue—was a hunter-gatherers' paradise. The Illini Indians called it "Sangamo" country, using a word meaning "land of plenty to eat," and the villagers called it the Eden of the West.

Zimri Enos, the son of Cox's business partner, became the county historian. He later wrote a description of Springfield in the 1820s for newcomers.

"Its beautiful location and surroundings...drained by never failing springs...beautiful groves of young forest trees of pin oak, elm, cherry and hackberry draped with grape vines and lined with plum, crabapples, hazel nuts and blackberries and encircled by millions of strawberry vines.

The heavy timber had an abundant supply of hickory nuts and walnuts and only the best were selected for the winter supply. We small boys used to gather May apples and dig ginseng, with the artichoke, were abundant. In the south was a pretty little sugar camp with quite a number of fine sugar trees. On the blue grass slope was the old Indian camp...they would go around to the best houses and dance. They were given bread, bacon, and corned beef, which they regarded as rarities and luxuries...

"Wild fruits, berries, and nuts brought the wild game and fowl of every sort, elk, deer, pheasants and wild turkey."[3]

Sangamon County was truly a paradise. But the Garden of Eden was stained by the ugly sin of slavery.

In practicality, slavery was not a clear and present danger in the state of Illinois except in the minds of the radicals and extremists and the fear they spread. Slavery was and is based on injustice and bad policy. However, there were only a few attempts

at plantations in early southern Illinois settlements. There were no slave markets in Illinois and absolutely no threats of a slave insurrection or revolt. The ironic truth of the issue was that there were never more than a thousand slaves registered or enumerated in state or federal census and the few slaves in Illinois were scattered over hundreds of square miles. Nevertheless, the presence of those few slaves proved to be too troublesome for this new state. Illinois was the perfect testing ground for the peaceful elimination of slavery. And Abraham Lincoln was one who would actively contribute to that peaceful evolution.

Everywhere Nance looked, she could see new log cabins being built. Trees fell daily, and foundation stones were pulled from the quarry to the west of town. Colonel Thomas Cox needed a large family home and built the finest two-story log house in the county. Beside his home he built an office building, later used by Asa Shaw and Cox's brother-in-law, Edward Mitchell. These two justices of the peace would later begin to write the permanent records of Nance's trials.

III

Thomas Cox went to work building his small empire with borrowed money and borrowed time. Across the road to the west, Cox built an ox mill for grinding corn and a whiskey distillery to make liquid gold for trade markets—but he started drinking too much of it himself. Colonel Cox used black slave labor and white hired men. Nance and Dice helped with the cooking. To build all of this, Thomas Cox borrowed lots and lots of money.

Colonel Cox became quite addicted to whiskey. Years later, Reverend William Salter, a circuit preacher said Cox "was a victim of *dipsomania,* and sometimes lost his head, of which weird stories are told."[4]

Dipsomania, an old term for alcoholism, is now considered to be an alcohol "blackout," when an addict can be functional but will remember little or nothing of what was said or done during a blackout episode.

Cox was a state bank director and was tempted to mismanage the funds. When the bank ran out of money, Cox borrowed five hundred dollars more from Sheriff John Taylor and even more money from the richest man in the county, a gun dealer named Nathaniel Cromwell, among others. Both Taylor and Cromwell later hired Lincoln when they needed a lawyer.

When the Illinois state bank failed in 1825, the governor learned that Colonel Cox had borrowed more money than state law allowed. Cox had also mismanaged the money of the Federal Land Office, and Congress fired him for misconduct.

Colonel Cox was reduced to the rank of private. Many of Thomas Cox's friends filed lawsuits to get back as much of the debt as they could by claiming Cox's properties, his home, his livestock, and even his human property in the form of two slaves, Nance and Dice. Cox was then struggling for the future of his family. His drinking episodes had the villagers laughing at him as the town drunk.

Enos noted, "there was great amount of talk and sympathy for Mrs. Cox and her five children. They were turned out of house and home, stripped of nearly everything, and compelled to take shelter in a little deserted log cabin a mile and a half from town."[5]

Keep in mind the key people all knew each other very well; they all had lived within a block of the center of the village. Among the first few families were young boys who had the run of the place and seemed to know everything that went on. Billy Herndon, Zimri Enos, and James Matheny would each grow up to become antislavery lawyers and friends of "Abram," as Lincoln was known in his younger days.

early
springfield:

PASFIELD

RUTLEDGE

KLEIN

FIRST

SECOND

THIRD

FOURTH

In the artist's sketch, the main street is Jefferson Avenue, shown from top to bottom of the page—west to east from Pasfield to Fourth Street. Cox's distillery was on Rutledge, while the ox mill was in the tree line near Klein. The Cox home was a two-story log cabin at the intersection of Jefferson and First Street. Sheriff John Taylor's family was diagonally across the street from the Cox house. Cromwell's gun shop was on the same block as Cox next to the courthouse, which was the Kelly cabin at Jefferson and Second Street. The Herndon family was across Second and two doors down from the corner, while the Enos house was at Jefferson and Third. Matheny's family was one block south of Cox's, along First Street. Thus all the principal characters lived within a block of the Kelly courthouse.[6]

The wealthy Nathaniel Cromwell Jr. wanted to claim the Cox home, while Sheriff Taylor sued to get Cox's ox mill and distillery. These men agreed to split Cox's real estate and slaves. Cromwell wanted Nance as a servant for his new young wife, Ann Eliza, and Taylor would take Nance's sister, Dice, to his home across the street.

However, Thomas Cox had been a scout and an Indian fighter since before the War of 1812. The governor feared trouble, so he appointed another tough Indian-fighter, John Howard, to serve as the county's coroner in order to help deal with Cox.

IV

During the first week of July 1827, Springfield held its traditional Fourth of July barbecue with speeches honoring freedom and liberty. But on Thursday, July 12, John Howard wrote on the back of a court order, "Came to hand at 7:00 a.m..."

Howard was ordered to seize Cox's slaves and property and hold an immediate auction. He began writing the first of many notes to which would become a very complicated eighteenth-month legal battle, he wrote some of the details directly on the court order as paraphrased below, but other details were sworn into testimonies that went all the way to the Illinois Supreme Court at Vandalia.

Neither Nance nor Dice had any prior warning of what was about to happen. They were to be auctioned off to Cromwell and

Taylor, and then Cox's cattle, oxen, and some land were sold. There is no record of whether Dice said nor did anything other than submit to her fate, but the same is not true of Nance. Nance protested, pulled to get away, and pleaded loudly, for the Cox family and the court could hear her cries for help.

According to court records, Nathan Cromwell purchased Nance for $151. He stepped up and "asked if Nance would go and live with him...Nance refused and persisted she would not. Cromwell told the coroner to take her to the old salt house." Howard tied her hands and shackled her feet and led Nance away for "six days" in the small, hot, steamy, and windowless shed. The community salt shed was used to preserve meat and fish; it was not intended as a prison. Meanwhile Dice was led away to the sheriff's house across the street.[7]

The next day, Nance's first full day of imprisonment in the hot, steamy storage shed, was the fortieth anniversary of the principle of July 13, 1787, in the Northwest Ordnance, that "Neither slavery nor involuntary servitude shall exist."

The following day, July 14, a messenger rode his horse hard all night to get to the little village. "Indians are attacking! Where's the sheriff?" shouted the governor's messenger.

The signal cannon fired. There was excitement in the street as guns and swords were drawn; mounted horsemen from all over the county rode to town to muster and march off to meet the Winnebago tribe more than a hundred miles away. The governor had ordered the state militia to mobilize for the Winnebago War in 1827. The militia mustered just outside the first courthouse, the old one-room Kelly cabin at Jefferson and Second, the same place where court ordered auctions were held.

Five companies of men, about five hundred from the county, left for a month to defend Galena, Illinois. There was no local danger except in the minds of the children and the wives, but the scare left Springfield almost a ghost town. Only the Cox family seemed to remain home, and Thomas knew he had to quit drinking and get sober.

Nance was still trapped in the salt shed! Terrified, hot, and sweating, she screamed to be let out. The sheriff and the coroner had completely forgotten about Nance!

Everyone who knew Nance seemed to like her. If the Indians had managed to bring the war to Sangamon County, that would have changed everything, so someone freed Nance from her confinement. And Nance went back to the Cox family, the only home she had ever known. The wealthy Cromwell did not have to serve in the militia; he went home to his wife in Sangamotown about seven miles away. And the county officials Taylor and Howard were exempt from mobilizing. When John Howard learned of Nance's "escape," he was furious!

For the sake of her grandchildren, Jane Cox had seen enough and got directly involved. Grandma Jane planned to buy back the family home in her name and with her money and open it as a boarding house. Her son, Thomas, hired a lawyer and filed a six-page appeal to get Nance back legally.

In September, Cox, with the assistance of his lawyer, filed formal charges against coroner John Howard for "Trespass by force and arms." Nance's trial was to be heard at the October term of the Sangamon Circuit Court, presided over by antislavery Supreme Court Justice Samuel Lockwood.

Since there were no other witnesses because of the Indian threat, nor any other confirming testimony, Thomas Cox possibly saw an opportunity to exaggerate the truth, as he sought to profit from Nance's pain.

V

"Nance, a Woman of Color, by her next friend
Thomas Cox v. John Howard."

This summarizes the charges still on file in supreme court archives in Springfield.

"Trespass; Assault; Battery, and false imprisonment...

One. Be it sworn that John Howard on the 24th day of July 1827 with force and arms made an assault upon the body of Nance at the house of Thomas Cox. With great violence ran upon her; then chased her about; then seized her; threw her down on the ground and with a fist; John pulled, dragged, forced and compelled Nance to the house of Sheriff Taylor. And there with a chain, bound and imprisoned her and kept her in prison for six days, where Nance was greatly exposed and injured.

Second. And John Howard made another assault on Nance; he laid hold and plucked, pulled the hair of Nance and with a fist struck Nance many violent blows about her head, face, breast, back, and legs and threw her down and with a chain bound her and violently kicked her. He next tore and damaged her clothes: one gown, one petty coat, one pair of stockings and one hand-kerchief: the value of twenty dollars. Nance was then sick for some time and remained so for eight weeks.

Third. Next, Nance suffered great pain and was prevented from doing her work. Nance was obliged and did pay out a large sum of money, forty dollars, in endeavoring to be cured of bruises, sickness, and disorders.

Fourth. John Howard on July 24 made another assault on Nance at the house of Thomas Cox in Springfield, Sangamon County. He beat and ill-treated Nance so much, her life was greatly despaired of...John Howard against the peace and dignity of the people of the state of Illinois and to the damages of Nance...Five Hundred dollars and therefore she, Nance, brings her suit.

Signed Thomas Cox for the Plaintiff"[8]

Nathaniel Cromwell Jr. was the wealthy son of a Baltimore aristocrat from the family of Oliver Cromwell of England. Nathaniel had been a major in Maryland during the War of 1812, and since moving his family to Illinois in 1824 he had become a land speculator, buying as much Illinois land as he could at low prices. He wanted Nance as a servant for his home to help his new, young wife, Ann Eliza.

Based on Thomas Cox's appeal and countersuit, Nathan Cromwell was commanded by the court to have Nance, a woman of color, before the judge at Springfield, with the cause of her detention.

In Sangamon Circuit Court, Friday 5 October 1827

Cromwell testified in the hearing of Nance v. Cromwell

"On June 24, 1825, Thomas Cox for $300.00, was paid by Nathan Cromwell, and sold to Cromwell the Negro girl, Nance as appears on deed of sale, marked 'A.'

And on November 21, 1826, Thomas Cox delivered to the possession of Cromwell, Nance, a girl of color.

Afterward, on July 12, 1827, on order from the clerk's office of the Circuit Court commanded the coroner of Sangamon County in favor of John Taylor, at the time the county sheriff, against the goods and lands of Thomas Cox.

The coroner exposed Nance to public sale to satisfy a debt, and Nathan Cromwell became the highest bidder of Nance for $151.00 dollars.

On the same day, Nance of her own free will and consent did agree and go with Cromwell where she still continues to live with Cromwell by her own choice."

Signed: Nathan Cromwell

Sworn before County Circuit Clerk Charles R. Matheny[9]

Charles Matheny was also an antislavery minister who had voted to abolish slavery at the first constitutional convention in Kaskaskia in 1818. Charles Matheny's son, James, became an antislavery lawyer and a friend of Abram Lincoln.

Irish Grandma Jane was a tough old lady, a petit blonde turned white. She was born in Virginia but raised her five kids in Kentucky while her husband, Robert Cox, also Irish, fought in the Indian wars of the 1790s. Now she would fight a different battle for her grandchildren's home and for Nance against the hated Englishman. Grandma Cox's testimony was unusual for this time in history since the business of law was not regarded as a proper place for women in the nineteenth century. It is noteworthy that the testimonies of Cromwell, Jane Cox and Nance were each given to different court officials. The court was being extra careful in handling this case.

Sworn testimony/deposition of Grandma Jane Cox to Justice of the Peace Asa Shaw, Saturday 6 October 1827:

"I say that Nance, the Negro girl, was raised from a child in the family of Thomas Cox in this state; that Nance was never out of the service of Thomas Cox's family until July.

I further say that after John Howard, the coroner, had taken Nance under court order, I saw Nance in Howard's custody confined with chains; Nance became very sick while thus confined.

I was there and I saw Howard sell Nance under the court order, that Cromwell became the purchaser. After which he asked Nance if she would go and live with him. Nance refused and persisted she would not.

Cromwell then told the coroner to take her back to where he brought her from.

Howard tied her and took her back to the old salt house.

After this Cromwell took her off. I am intimate in the family of Thomas Cox, and I am fully satisfied Nance was not out of our service before last July when she was sold by court order.

I further say I have heard Nance repeatedly protest against going to live with or to serve Cromwell, and also protest against remaining in his service."

Her

Jane "X" Cox[10]

Mark

[These court depositions have been edited and paraphrased to eliminate redundancies and archaic legal terms. Court papers at the time were penned and witnessed by clerks and prepared so that uneducated witnesses need only sign testimonies by their mark of an "X."]

The Cox family was using their knowledge of Illinois law to defeat Cromwell. Thomas Cox was a state senator when Illinois legalized the softer, gentler black laws of indentured servitude that required the legal "consent" of the servant by a signed contract for clothing, room, and board, which was totally unheard of in the slave states. The Coxes hoped Nance's protests and sympathy of the court would make her free to return to the only family she had ever known. This testimony would have been impossible in most states. It was singularly historic that a black servant testified in a white man's court in the 1820s.

One of Cromwell's forefathers, Oliver Cromwell, had sponsored the Petition of Right in England two hundred years before, in 1628. The petition was intended to curtail royal abuse of power by giving specific *civil rights* to loyal subjects. It was both historic and poetic justice that an English nobleman was commanded into an American courtroom to answer the charges of an African American female servant.

And Nance would call the gentleman Nathaniel Cromwell a liar!

The language in the heading of the original historic document is the first hint that there is some confusion in the court whether Nance should be considered a girl or tried as an adult woman.

State of Illinois—Sangamon County Circuit Court October term, 1827

Nance, a Negro girl v. Nathan Cromwell

One. It is not true! I swear it is not true...that Thomas Cox gave me to the possession of Cromwell; nor did I ever live with him nor serve him until I was delivered to Cromwell by John Howard in July last and which was against my will and consent. And delivery of me, Nance, to Cromwell was not until after I was sold under court order for debt and taxes by Howard as property.

Two. It is not true that I, Nance, voluntarily and of my own free will, agreed to go with Cromwell to his house in Sangamotown; nor is it true I still live with Cromwell by my own choice.

Three. She (Nance) never before or since made any contract with Cromwell and is now detained and restrained of her personal liberty against her will and consent.

She prays the court to order a further trial, as may be just and right, and conduct a full and fair hearing of this cause, which she hopes to be discharged and released from the illegal restraint of Cromwell.

Her

Negro "X" Nance[11]

Mark

Read as Her Mark, "X," Negro Nance.

Signed, sealed: Justice of the Peace Edward Mitchell, Saturday 6 October 1827.

John Howard did not testify in court, nor did he deny the charges of assault and battery. But his lawyer, John Reynolds, a future governor, rebutted with the claim that Howard was only following instructions of the court order and used "...no more force than necessary."[12]

VI

*N*ance's trials were referred to the December 1827 term of the Illinois State Supreme Court. *Nance Cox, a Woman of Color v. John Howard,* 1827, had become a high-profile slavery case. The historic trial was to be championed by the state's leading antislavery against proslavery advocates. The antislavery men included former governor Edward Coles, supreme court justice Samuel Lockwood, and the court clerk Reverend Charles Matheny. Thomas Cox's lawyer was Samuel McRoberts, a future US senator, and Howard's lawyer was future governor John Reynolds. Both had served as proslavery judges, and both had owned slaves.

Justice Samuel Lockwood asked a simple but important question in law: "How old was Nance?" By law Nance must have reached the age of legal consent, just like in a marriage contract, or she would have to be treated by the court as an orphaned child.

Jane Cox had said Nance was a teenager but did not say if Nance had reached the age of legal consent. Howard told Justice

Lockwood that Nance's records would be found in the old capitol, Kaskaskia, over a hundred miles away. Lockwood had no choice but to delay the trial a year to get proof of Nance's birth in the state of Illinois and her actual age. Meanwhile, Nance lived in the Taylor household while they awaited the appeal.

Justice Lockwood's edited preliminary notes in 1827, were never handed down as a verdict of the supreme court, but showed he wanted to free Nance.

> "…(Nance) Plaintiff replied, 'She is not…property liable by the law…to be taken and sold…'"
> First, No law of this state authorizes the sale…of servants. Do the Acts (of the General Assembly) make them goods or real estate? Most certainly neither…"
> To serve whom? Surely not the highest bidder for them at Sheriff's sale *without their consent, (emphasis added)*. 2nd … There is no law of the state authorizing the sale of Negroes, that they cannot be sold…" *Cox v Howard, Archives; case 156.*

However, Lockwood had to consider conflicting laws; Nance's age; fairness to Taylor and Cromwell who lost money; and to collect Cox's back taxes. So the complicating laws forced the Justice to forward the case to the full Illinois Supreme Court docketed as *"Nance a girl of Color v. John Howard"* in December 1828.

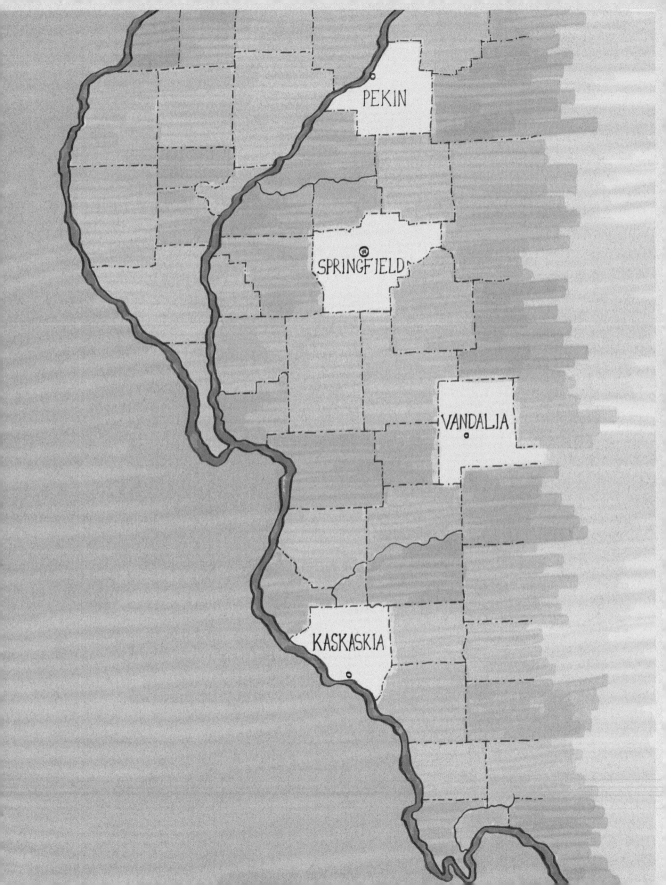

VII

Old records of the Underground Railroad show that fugitive slaves crossed the Ohio River near Pigeon Creek and Anderson Creek, where Abraham Lincoln worked as a teenager. Runaway slaves were hunted by slave chasers with dogs in those areas. Lincoln was familiar with the cruel hunting methods used by slave chasers and bounty hunters and hated their brutality. He developed a lifelong hatred of slave chasers.[13]

During the autumn of 1828, Abram Lincoln and Allen Gentry made a riverboat trip to New Orleans to sell the fall harvest of Gentryville, Indiana. At night they would tie the boat to shore before sleeping. One night, Lincoln went onto the main deck to check a suspicious noise. Lincoln suddenly ducked his head just in time to miss a deathblow from a club-swinging runaway slave trying to kill him for his food. Lincoln was severely cut on the scalp fighting seven starving slaves who were there to rob and kill just two men.[14]

Both Midwestern farmhands were country wrestlers, tall and strong enough to throw weakened slaves with just one arm. Lincoln grabbed his favorite tool, a sharp, double-edged ax, and cut the tie rope with one swing. Whether Lincoln then turned the ax toward the slaves is simply not mentioned in the accounts, but the starving slaves retreated into the water. Along the backwater, the wounded men did not know where to find medical treatment, and if they did, they might not have had enough money. Head wounds left unstitched leave prominent scars, and Lincoln felt those scars in his hairline for a very long time to come. With his heart thumping from the excitement of the fight, and the painful throbbing of his right temple made his muscled fingers shaky and pulsating as the men tried first aid for each other in unsanitary conditions.

So, by the time of *Nance (Cox), a girl of color v. Howard*, December 1828, both Nance and Abraham Lincoln shared something in common. They were both permanently scarred and shaken by the violence of slavery!

VIII

When John Howard returned from his fact-finding journey to Kaskaskia, he had learned that Nance had been born in the Illinois Territorial Capitol building in 1813 while the Territorial Assembly was meeting in Cox's boarding house. Nance's father, Randol Legins, died about 1817, and Thomas Cox sold Nance's mother, Anachy, to a Kentucky lawyer in 1820. Nance was legally an orphan child.[15]

When auctioned, beaten, and jailed by John Howard, Nance was just thirteen years old!

The four supreme court justices were divided on slavery; two voted yea, and two voted nay. After all the legal rationalizing, the final verdict was that a servant was a possession "and *can be sold*" on order of a court. Nance Cromwell remained a slave to the Cromwell family by court order.

Sadly, Justice Lockwood realized he could not free Nance, because she would be an easy victim of slave chasers or bounty hunters who would sell her downriver. She had to live in the home of a white, male head of household, if only as protection from worse slavery conditions south of the Ohio River. And Thomas Cox might try to mortgage her again, so Nance lost her plea.

More importantly, the supreme court ruling established a solid legal basis for indentured servitude to continue in a free state, and that ruling would go unchallenged and unchanged for the next ten years. So Nance lost her bid for freedom, and the court ordered her to remain Cromwell's servant, at least until the age of eighteen years, the age for legal marriage.[16]

IX

By this time, Cromwell had moved again and was living temporarily on the Gideon Hawley farm near Peoria, in Tazewell County. Cromwell had hired a new college-trained lawyer, John Stuart, a lifelong friend of Abraham Lincoln.

Nathaniel Cromwell formed a new business partnership with David Bailey. As a result of Nance's work for the Cromwell family, Nathan had more time to buy up land as a speculator and build the new town of Pekin, named by his wife Ann Eliza. The two men worked together as town trustees, worked on the railroad committee, and established the streets and town boundaries with village attorney John Stuart.

Major David Bailey served with Captain Abraham Lincoln during the Black Hawk War in 1832. After the war, Major Bailey married Sarah Brown in November while visiting Fort Dearborn; she was the daughter of Rufus Brown, an early conductor of the Underground Railroad in Chicago. Bailey and Lincoln became political friends when Lincoln became the Whig Party organizer for Illinois while Bailey was a Whig leader in Tazewell County. Cromwell was busy building a hotel and another town nine miles east of Pekin called Tremont. Nance was busy making lasting friendships with the women folk of both towns. The young pioneering wives had no midwife to help with birthing, child illnesses, and other women's labor. Nance had experience in those skills from Grandma Jane and Mrs. Roba Cox's five children.[17]

The end of the Black Hawk War in 1832 marked the start of a long period of deadly events. Nance's hometown was infected with three disease epidemics. Cholera came downriver with the returning soldiers and then spread back upriver again two years later. As many as half the settlers sickened and died; others contracted the lifelong disease of malaria or other maladies. Eventually, riverboats refused to stop at Pekin out of fear of disease. When young Mrs. Cromwell died by 1834, Nathan was very depressed and decided to leave, but he would not take Nance.

Nance was frightened when she learned Cromwell was moving again, this time to the slave state of Texas. It was during this development Nance decided to have her first child at the age of twenty-three. She had cooked for the white men and free or indentured black hired men working on Cromwell's many building projects. In the spring of 1836, Nance began to show she was going to have a baby soon, thus complicating any plans for moving on a long journey. Nathan Cromwell was sixty-four years old and traveling with a single, black twenty-three year old slave who was a mother-to-be would attract too much unwanted attention. So Nance would stay in Illinois, but it was illegal for Cromwell to abandon her; he had to make some legal arrangements. What had to be done?

Hurrying to catch the next riverboat down the Illinois River, Cromwell stopped at Bailey's store and made a hasty deal for Nance to stay with the Bailey family. David Bailey would agree to a young pregnant woman working in his store only if Mrs. Sarah Bailey agreed to the arrangement. So it was unlikely that either old Cromwell or young Bailey was the father of Nance's child. Unfortunately, white, male centered nineteenth century history seldom records what wives or other women said or did in these matters. A businessman signed as witness that the Baileys agreed to pay about four hundred dollars for Nance's services for one year until Cromwell returned.

X

Nathan Cromwell never came back. Disease had weakened him; he became ill on the riverboat and died a month later. When news reached Pekin in August that Nathan was dead, Nance must have remembered something said during her previous trials and insisted she was now a free woman.

There was new slavery trouble brewing throughout Illinois with the assassination of Abolitionist publisher Reverend E.P. Lovejoy. In 1837, there was a statewide call for an Abolition Petition, in spite of threats against it, and signed by 245 intrepid anti-slavery men including David Bailey, who had family ties to the Underground Railroad.

This led to riots in at least four Illinois cities including the new capitol at Springfield. Future Governor John Palmer witnessed

several violent incidents, from his autobiographical, *Personal Recollections of...* p. 23, near the riverboat town of Naples.

"I saw that the street...was crowded with people...a number of persons were kicking and striking a man...and was told that several men had followed the stranger who had lectured the night before, pulled him off his horse and had taken his petition from him, and were then pursuing every man who had signed it to compel him to take his name off the paper...(A)bout four o'clock, found the streets full of people, and learned that they had driven Mr. Ozias Hatch, afterwards Secretary of the State of Illinois, into the belfry of the Baptist Church, in which he took refuge to avoid the mob, and that they were still in pursuit of others who had signed the petition."

David Bailey signed a petition to abolish slavery and would not force a young mother to work, but he refused to pay Cromwell's estate the money Bailey had promised to pay on the bank note. Nathan's son, Dr. William Cromwell, filed suit in probate court. These actions led to Nance's next trial *Cromwell v. Bailey* 1838. During this time, there was another bank failure, and Bailey fell into financial crisis. David Bailey lost the trial in 1839. He then

hired his wartime comrade-in-arms Abraham Lincoln to appeal the verdict to the state supreme court.[18]

When Abraham Lincoln filed papers for the appeal, Nance Legins-Cromwell became the only African American servant whose freedom cause was appealed three times in the Illinois Supreme Court. Lawyers knew that Nance's status in court would be more respectable to the justices if she was a married woman since, by that time, she had two infant girls.

So in October 1840, just two weeks after Lincoln had visited Pekin as part of his circuit law practice, Nance legally married Benjamin Costley, a free black man from Illinois, before a justice of the peace. In 1840 it was commonly believed among lawyers that it was impossible to win a slavery case, because the laws were overwhelmingly against African Americans. Moreover, most lawyers refused "Negro cases," because they were damaging to their professional reputation. So Nance was doubly blessed to have Lincoln, who agreed to work as her advocate and at the same time help his friend David Bailey, who teetered on bankruptcy. The case of *Cromwell v. Bailey*, 1838 began in the Tazewell County courthouse in Tremont.

Abraham Lincoln was inspired by seven words of his favorite founding father, Thomas Jefferson, "Neither slavery nor involuntary servitude shall exist...." Lincoln knew he needed to emphasize his pleadings so the justices would not miss his main argument. Lincoln's study and research showed him that that key phrase appeared in Illinois law three times: in 1787, in 1809, and again in the state constitution of 1818. So Lincoln composed his case around repeating that phrase three times to be sure the justices focused on that idea.

Before 1840, most lawyers believed slavery cases were impossible to win due to the tough laws. Lincoln got some encouragement from some recent news. In March 1841, newspapers nationwide printed headlines that John Quincy Adams won the case of *United States v. Amistad*, a famous slavery case, just four months before Nance's trial.

Twenty years before, back in 1822, Nance's master Thomas Cox quit the Illinois Senate to become chairman of the Convention Committee; his plan was to make Illinois a perpetual slave state by constitutional amendment. As Cox planned and directed the strategies of a most heated, and at times violent, campaign through 1823 and 1824, Cox had no reason to believe his then ten-year-old domestic servant could possibly pose a threat to his long-term objective. However, the ear has no choice but to hear, and years later, Nance, with the help of Lincoln, would ultimately prove Thomas Cox wrong.

XI

To add to the moral weight of a slavery case, court was to be held in a house of God. The new capitol dome was not yet finished, and the supreme court was held in rented space in the new St. Paul's Episcopal Church, just a few blocks from where Nance had been auctioned in 1827.

In practice, lawyers talk with all those involved. White scar tissue on black skin is quite an obvious sight. This could create a bond. Nance's severe beating, "...about her head, face, breast..." surely left marks. Nance's scars plus the facts she was again a pregnant mother were more than enough to gain the sympathy of lawyer Lincoln who had his own scars from the inherent violence of slavery.

Two weeks before the Alton rioting in 1837, the domestic tranquility in Springfield had been so disrupted it split the

Presbyterian congregation in two. The church literally became God's house –- divided. A public meeting led by Supreme Court Justice Thomas Browne condemned the doctrine of immediate emancipation stating, "The efforts of abolitionists in this community are neither necessary nor useful." Illinois was becoming a state divided.

As Lincoln waited in the church for court to begin, his fingers quivered with tension from the nervousness he felt about his first Illinois Supreme Court session. In addition, he was arguing this case against Steven Logan, his new law partner from the slave state of Kentucky. Logan was thought of as the best lawyer in the state, and there were new justices in this court Lincoln didn't know very well. It was hot and humid on July 9, and Lincoln was sweating. But if he could win this trial, he thought it might eventually help to free the thousand slaves in Illinois by challenging the interpretation of the old laws. Lincoln wiped his face dry again and again felt the jagged scar under his hairline. He remembered the permanent lash scars and the looks of lifelong cruelty in the faces of those seven starving slaves who had tried to kill him for his food. Lincoln was suddenly startled by the sound of the gavel striking an echo in the church. Nance's trial had begun.

The trial as summarized here was called *Bailey v. Cromwell*. Lincoln argued for Bailey and Nance that the debt was not legal; that no value was received from the sale; that the note was given for the purchase of a slave when Nance was, in fact and in law, a free woman; and that Cromwell had promised to show papers of proof, but there was no contract offering proof.[19]

Abraham Lincoln used ten legal references to sway the court. Of these cases four were antislavery trials from other states, and three were laws repeated from Illinois. The first two points of law referred to the tricky logic of contract law prepared with the help of Stephen Logan. Next, Lincoln turned to his talents of concise brevity and clarity of principle. Lincoln tailored his speech toward uneducated country juries. Lincoln's delivery became known for its simplicity and was so persuasively spoken as to become eloquent.

The three Illinois laws each restated the seven words of the Northwest Ordinance of July 13, 1787 that: "Neither slavery nor involuntary servitude shall exist..." in Illinois, the territory or the state.

The ultimate question Lincoln put before the justices to decide was "who had the burden of proof, the supposed master or the alleged slave?" By July 23, 1841, the court had reached a verdict and handed down new precedents into Illinois law that "in the absence of proof presumption that she was free must prevail."[20]

> "It is a presumption of law, in the state of Illinois, that every person is free, without regard to color.
>
> (And, therefore...) The sale of a free person is illegal." (Still enforced in the twenty-first century).[21]

Abraham Lincoln had been a lawyer for less than five years and at age thirty-two was still a junior partner, but Lincoln had won the court decision and at the same time impressed the eight justices presiding over the case.

Nance was free! After fifteen years of fears, hopes and appeals,

Nance was free! After fifteen years of fears, hopes, and appeals, Nance was free at last!

XII

$\mathcal{N}$ ance Legins-Costley, (1813-1873), had been a slave by legal definition under a court order. In the case of *Nance v. Howard*, 1828, the verdict read, "A servant is a possession and *can be sold*." Abraham Lincoln swayed the court to declare the sale of a person was illegal. Nance and her first three of eight children were born as slaves but were henceforth and forever free twenty years before the Civil War.

A friend of Lincoln's, Isaac Arnold had been a supreme court clerk in 1841, he had just gotten promoted to supreme court lawyer; he likely witnessed the case of *Bailey v Cromwell*. Arnold later wrote, "It is believed that no attempt has since been made to sell a human being in the state of Illinois." He was the only Lincoln biographer who was there. In Arnold's writings and speeches he believed the Trials of Nance started Lincoln on the path that changed American history.[22]

Nance's trials became a watershed case, meaning the case opened the doors of all the courts in the state to more slavery cases. And other lawyers repeated and reused Lincoln's work for Nance's trial to win other slavery cases at least six times in the next ten years.

About the time *Bailey v. Cromwell* started in 1837, the American Antislavery Society adopted as its symbol the Liberty Bell of Philadelphia and the slogan, "Let Freedom Ring!"

When the court finished its work on Nance's trials and the jurists were walking home for the day, the church bells of Saint Paul's began to chime. The bells seemed to ring a little louder that day. The joyful chime seemed to ring clearly, declaring liberty for all of Illinois. The chimes seemed to echo sixty miles north, where Nance learned neither she nor her children would ever have to fear being shackled and locked in a lawn shed again.

Epilogue

In less than five years, the Illinois Supreme Court ruled that all forms of slavery were outlawed. In 1848, the people of Illinois voted to make slavery unconstitutional in the state. The census of 1850 showed that not one of the thousand servants were still slaves. In less than ten years, Illinois peacefully abolished slavery!

The historic significance of the "Trials of Nance" was that Nance represented the legal personification of the definition of slavery over thirteen years and three supreme court appeals. The *Nance v Howard, 1828* verdict read, "A servant is a possession and CAN BE SOLD." The *Bailey v Cromwell, 1841* decision was "...every person is free without regard to color." And therefore, "The sale of a free person is illegal." This is still enforced in the 21st century. Nance Legins-Costley, circa 1813-1873, has earned a place in US history as the first slave freed by Abraham Lincoln and as an early African-American pioneer and a human rights advocate. Nance's case history defined, tested, and ultimately broke indentured servitude as a disguise for slavery.

More than twenty years later, Abraham Lincoln successfully signed into federal law those famous, now eternal, seven words he used so well in the trials of Nance "Neither slavery nor involuntary servitude shall exist..." in any of the remaining US territories in 1862.

Then Abraham Lincoln began composing the Emancipation Proclamation, in which he said that his whole soul was in it. Many people from all walks of life congratulated Lincoln so many times the day he was to sign the Emancipation Proclamation that his hands were quivering from shaking hundreds of hands. Indeed by 1865, the Civil War had prematurely aged Lincoln. He was thinner, and his hands appeared thin-skinned and bony, but he was as strong as ever.

Nance's story shows Abraham Lincoln was consistent from first to last in his moral, professional and legal belief embodied in his historical legacy of the Thirteenth Amendment to the Constitution of the United States --- the last best hope of earth that "Neither slavery nor involuntary servitude shall exist..." anywhere.

When Lincoln sat down to sign the Thirteenth Amendment, beginning with, "Neither slavery nor involuntary servitude shall exist…" he did not think that it would be the last constitutional act of his life. Lincoln stretched his arm, combed his long fingers through his hair, and suddenly froze in thought for a moment when he realized he could no longer feel the scar under his hair. Abraham Lincoln smiled, his hands calmed, and with his firm, steady signature, the scar of the violence of slavery was gone.

Triumphantly, Nance Legins-Costley was quoted in Tazewell County history, "All my (eight) children were born in freedom" --- in the land of Lincoln.

No one wrote a better legacy of Nance's worthiness to her community than the local newspaper publisher William Bates. In 1870, the paper published the "City Directory." At the top of page ten was a glowing tribute to Nance Legins (Cox Cromwell) Costley circa 1813-1873 a well-known, good neighbor.

> "With the arrival of Major Cromwell, the head of the company that afterwards purchased the land upon which Pekin is built, came a slave. That slave still lives in Pekin and is now known, as she has been known for nearly a half a century, by the citizens of Pekin, "Black Nancy." She came here a chattel, with "no rights that a white man was bound to respect." For more than forty years she has been known here as a "negro" upon whom there was no discount, and her presence and services have been indispensable on many a select occasion. But she has outlived the era of barbarism, and now, in her still vigorous old age, she sees her race disenthralled; the chains that bound them forever broken, their equality before the law everywhere recognized and her children enjoying the elective franchise. A chapter in the history of a slave and in the progress of a nation."

History of the phrase: "Neither Slavery nor Involuntary Servitude shall exist..."

1784:   Thomas Jefferson's proposal to Congress, defeated by one vote.

1787:   Nathan Dane's Article VI to the Northwest Ordinance passed.

1841:   A. Lincoln: *Bailey v. Cromwell*, Supreme Court argued against servitude in Illinois by repeating this history three times.

           1787:   Ordinance of Congress as applied to northern Midwest.

           1809:   Northwest Ordinance as applied to Illinois Territory.

           1818:   Northwest Ordinance as applied to Illinois State constitution.

1846–49:   David Wilmot Proviso; Congressman Lincoln voted for it forty times but never passed.

1848:   Illinois's second constitution based on state supreme court rulings.

1862:   Signed by A. Lincoln, prohibited in all US territories.

1865:   Signed Abraham Lincoln, Thirteenth Amendment: "Neither slavery nor involuntary servitude shall exist..." became the supreme law of the land.

Postscript

Nance and Benjamin Costley's oldest son, William Henry was born in September 1840 while Nance still awaited Lincoln's court appeal. Bill grew up along the Pekin-Peoria Illinois road; the same road Lawyer Lincoln traveled several times every year. Nance's eight children played along that road as they grew up. With Nance's gratitude toward Lincoln the kids probably knew him by name. Bill eventually made a living taking care of white men's horses, even Lincoln's, but unlike his enslaved cousins, Bill worked as a free man.

Bill was 20 years when the Civil War erupted, but Negro men could not enlist. By 1863 there had been draft riots across the Illinois river in Fulton and Peoria, so President Lincoln actively recruited black soldiers and sailers.

Enlisting in 1864 was an act of raw courage. Pvt. Wm H. Corsley (his illiteracy left his name misspelled in war records) joined the 29th Regt. US Colored Infantry, just weeks after the Battle of the Crater where racial atrocities peaked. Hundreds of African Americans, including the Illinois 29th had been trapped on the battlefield and summarily executed. The Illinois Regt. suffered 70% casualties. Bill and dozens of other Africans joined to reinforce the decimated unit. During the final battle for Petersburg, Bill was wounded in the shoulder forcing him to spend the last week of the war in the hospital.

However, Pvt. Bill Costley was not through making Black History yet. He recovered and rejoined the 29th of Illinois, which was sent to Texas as the original "Buffalo Soldiers". While in route by sea, a storm forced his troop ship to seek safe harbor and resupply at Galveston. When army work details from the ships reported that black longshoremen were still enslaved, Gen. Gordon Granger with his armed Colored Soldiers threatened martial law and decreed "...all slaves are free." This erupted into the history making celebration known as "Juneteenth"; witnessed and participated by the first male slave freed by Lincoln 25 years before, William Henry Costley (1840-1888) – a moment of history.

For more see <www.nancebook.com>

Further Reading: A Bibliography

Adams, Carl. "The First Slave Freed by Abraham Lincoln: A Biographical Sketch of Nance Legins-Costley." *For The People,* Autumn 1999, p.1.

———. "Lincoln's First Freed Slave: A Review of *Bailey v. Cromwell, 1841" Journal of Illinois State Historical Society,* Vol. 101; *Lincoln Bicentennial,* 2008, p. 235,259.

Blockson, Charles, *The Underground Railroad,* Berkley Books, New York, 1987.

Zimri Enos; "Description of Springfield"; Illinois Historical Transactions #14; Springfield, 1909.

Foner, Eric; *The Fiery Trial*; W. W. Norton, New York; 2010, p. 47.

Harris, N. Dwight, *History of Negro Servitude in Illinois*, Chicago, 1904.

Sandberg, Carl, *Abraham Lincoln: The Prairie Years*, Harcourt Brace, New York; 1926.

Warren, Louis, *Lincoln's Youth*. Indiana Historical Society, Indianapolis; 1959, p. 184.

There are many Lincoln biographies. Biographies of many people in this book can be found online.

A Note to Parents and Teachers about the First Slave Freed by Abraham Lincoln

This work is based on a true biographical story of Nance Legins-Costley, 1813–1873, who was born in Illinois, a supposed "free state." In the nation's history, there were only two "indentured servitude" states, Indiana and Illinois, thanks to William H. Harrison. Lincoln lived in both these states. Lincoln's first law book, *Indiana Territorial Laws*, still exists, and the famous Northwest Ordinance of Congress of 1787, as one of the first original American laws, was published at the beginning of the volume.

After twelve years of search and research, the story is still incomplete. There is no evidence of who released Nance from confinement or exactly where Nance lived as a ward of the court between August 1827 and December 1828. Very little is known of Nance's husband, Benjamin Costley, including where he lived before 1840. Many, many questions remain unanswered. It is easy to believe Nance's name was pronounced "Nancy," but all records except one show her named spelled as "Nance."

There is a social theory that each person has only six degrees of separation from famously important people. Most of the people in this work show they had only one degree of separation from Abraham Lincoln, such as the Springfield boys Billy Herndon, Zimri Enos, and James Matheny, who all knew about Nance and later became lawyers and friends of Lincoln after Cromwell and Nance had moved out of Springfield.

This story concerns just three recurring themes all documented and based on facts. The "slave girl named Nance" had more handwritten documents about her trials than any other black female servant in nineteenth-century Illinois courts, including an unprecedented three supreme court appeals.

Lincoln had a personal hatred of slavery and slave chasers, but the story of his lifelong scar from near murder at age nineteen by desperately hungry men is often forgotten or ignored. When I ask people about scars on their faces or heads, they know exactly when, where, and how they were scarred. Why wouldn't Lincoln remember this since he was also sensitive about his appearance?

The third recurring theme is the historic, now eternal, phrase: "Neither slavery nor involuntary servitude shall exist." It is a curious coincidence that the proof of Lincoln's convictions was in a trilogy of trilogies, in that all the important elements of this historic story added up to three separate incidents. Lincoln first used those words legally to free

Nance and then later to free all of the United States' slaves. These are the only words the United States ever went to war over.

    Carl Adams, 2014

Index of Persons:

About the author

Carl Michael Adams (1951-20--) was born and raised in Alton, Illinois, and has been a lifelong fan of Abraham Lincoln. Carl Adams grew up near the permanent monument to abolitionist publisher Elisha Parish Lovejoy, who was killed by a mob during an antiabolition riot in his hometown. Carl earned a bachelor's degree in broadcast journalism from Southern Illinois University at Edwardsville in 1979. He worked for more than twenty years on Public Radio documentaries and network television news and is now semiretired. In the 1970s and 1980s, Carl lectured as a military training officer for both the marines and the army in the art and sciences of communications, including lessons of military history.

In his project called the "Trials of Nance," Adams had to dig deep into Lincoln and Illinois history to recover the story of the first slave freed by Abraham Lincoln, a story that for over a hundred years was lost to history.